reflections *on solitude*

October 2000

reflections
on solitude

To Joan,

with much love,

Vidyādevī

WINDHORSE PUBLICATIONS

Published by Windhorse Publications
11 Park Road
Birmingham
B13 8AB

© Windhorse Publications 2000

Cover photo Devamitra
Design Marlene Eltschig
Printed by Interprint Limited, Malta

A catalogue record for this book is available
from the British Library

ISBN 1 899579 28 1

contents

1   Introduction

5   The Lake Isle of Innisfree

7   Advice to a Young Poet

9   The Joys of Solitude

10 I Saw in Louisiana a Live-Oak Growing

12 The Daffodils

14 Zarathustra's Down-going

16 The Tree-Rootman's Practice

17 Aloneness

20 No News

21 A Solitary Retreat

23 Bamboo Grove House

24 Sufficient Space

28 Solitude

30 The Happiness of Solitude. The Hermit´s History

36 The Story of Asanga

39 Parting at Morning

40 Himalayan Sages

42 A Life of Special Love

44 Entering the Dark Wood

46 Wishing for a Companion

47 These Mornings of Rain

50 Choices

52 Conditions for Meditation

53 We *are* Solitary

acknowledgements

The publishers wish to acknowledge with gratitude permission to quote from the following:

p.5: 'The Lake Isle of Innisfree' from W.B. Yeats, *Selected Poetry*, ed. A. Norman Jeffares, Pan Books in association with Macmillan, London 1974. Reproduced by permission of A.P. Watt Ltd, on behalf of Michael B. Yeats. Also reprinted with the permission of Scribner, a division of Simon & Schuster from *The Collected Poems of W.B. Yeats*, Revised second edition by Richard J. Finneran. Copyright © 1983, 1989 by Anne Yeats.

p.9: *Four Huts: Asian Writings on the Simple Life*, by Kamo no Chomei, translated by Burton Watson, copyright 1994. Reprinted by arrangement with Shambhala Publications Inc., Boston, www.shambhala.com

p.14: *Thus Spoke Zarathustra: A Book for Everyone and No One*, by Friedrich Nietzsche, translated by R.J. Hollingdale (Penguin Classics, 1961) copyright R.J. Hollingdale, 1961, 1969.

p.16: *The Path of Purification* (Visuddhimagga), translated by Bhikkhu Nanamoli, Buddhist Publication Society, Kandy 1991.

p.20: *One Robe, One Bowl: The Zen Poetry of Ryokan*, translated by John Stevens, published by Weatherhill, New York/Tokyo 1977.

p.36: *The Door of Liberation: Essential Teachings of the Tibetan Buddhist Tradition*, translated by Geshe Wangyal, Wisdom Publications, Boston 1995.

p.42: *Contemplation in a World of Action*, by Thomas Merton, published by George Allen and Unwin Ltd, London 1971, reproduced by permission of Routledge and the Merton Legacy Trust.

p.44: *Poems of Early Buddhist Nuns* (Therigatha), translated by
Mrs C.A.F. Rhys Davids and K.R. Norman, PTS, Oxford
1997. Reproduced with permission from the Pali Text
Society who own the copyright.

p.46: *Cold Mountain*, trans. Burton Watson © 1970 Columbia
University Press. Reprinted by permission of the
publisher.

p.47: 'These Mornings of Rain' from *Horses Make a Landscape
More Beautiful, Poems by Alice Walker,* copyright © 1984 by
Alice Walker, reprinted by permission of Harcourt, Inc.,
and David Higham Associates Ltd. Published by Women's
Press. London 1985.

p.50: 'Choices' from Elizabeth Jennings, *Collected Poems*, published by Carcanet Press Ltd, Manchester, 1987. Reprinted
with permission of David Higham Associates Ltd.

p.52: *A Buddhist Bible*, edited by Dwight Goddard, Beacon Press
Books, Boston 1970, reproduced by arrangement with E.P.
Dutton & Co. Inc.

p.53: Rainer Maria Rilke, *Letters to a Young Poet*, translated and
with a foreword by Stephen Mitchell, published by Vintage
Books, Random House, New York, 1986. Reprinted by
permission of Random House and Insel Verlag.

Every effort has been made to trace copyright in the following, but
if any omission has been made let let us know in order that this may
be acknowledged in the next edition.

p.23: 'Bamboo Grove House' from Poems of Wang Wei, translated with an introduction by G.W. Robinson, originally
published in the periodical *Art & Literature*, Penguin, UK 1973.

For my mother, whose love of literature –
and of solitude – first inspired my own

INTRODUCTION

I put this anthology together at the invitation of a friend who wanted to explore the experience of solitude as reflected in the spiritual and literary traditions of both East and West. When I came to consider the word solitude, I was interested to find that its connotations are (as it seemed to me) entirely positive – as distinct from 'loneliness', which has very different associations. In this collection you will find many people rejoicing in a solitary life, or in the kind of brief period of solitude that comes as a welcome relief in the midst of busyness, while others confront, or quail at, the more challenging aspects of a life lived alone. Some writings reflect on the existential fact of aloneness, while through others the spiritual benefits to be derived from solitude shine, and yet others explore the relationship of a solitary life to a sense of connectedness with others.

Such a short collection can only be a very personal selection, and I have enjoyed the meditation on solitude that its creation has involved. I have especially appreciated the opportunity to bring together the reflections of many times and places on this theme.

I hope this book will provide inspiration during periods of solitude – voluntary or otherwise – and the opportunity for solitary interludes that reading gives even in the midst of the busiest of lives. As Yeats suggests in the first poem of the collection, in our imagination we can always 'arise and go to Innisfree'.

Vidyadevi

THE LAKE ISLE OF INNISFREE

I will arise and go now, and go to Innisfree,
And a small cabin build there, of clay and
   wattles made:
Nine bean-rows will I have there, a hive for
   the honey-bee,
And live alone in the bee-loud glade.

And I shall have some peace there, for
   peace comes dropping slow,
Dropping from the veils of the morning to
   where the cricket sings;
There midnight's all a glimmer, and noon a
   purple glow,
And evening full of the linnet's wings.

I will arise and go now, for always night
   and day
I hear lake water lapping with low sounds
   by the shore;

While I stand on the roadway, or on the
    pavements grey,
I hear it in the deep heart's core.

W.B. Yeats

ADVICE TO A YOUNG POET

Without some degree of solitude reflection is impossible, and without prolonged reflection no great work of art was ever brought forth. The poet needs solitude as the lungs need air. By Solitude is meant not so much physical loneliness as inner isolation, for the time being at least, from all that does not directly concern the process of poetic creation. Physical withdrawal from normal human activities and interests can be included in the definition of solitude only to the extent that the latter is dependent on it. In the urbanized and industrialized societies of the present age this is with increasing frequency the case. Without withdrawing externally from the hurry and bustle of modern life the poet may not be able to find the internal solitude necessary for the progress and perfection of his work. At the same time, the necessity of earning his own livelihood – on its own level a no less urgent problem – again and again draws him from solitude back into society.

In a world wherein Poetry as a profession is no longer recognized or remunerated, the young poet has to find a way of life which will enable him to provide for both the lower and higher necessities of his nature.

The religious mystic, to whom opportunities for solitude are as necessary as to the poet, can find them in the solemn hush of monastery or hermitage; but corresponding facilities are not offered by an indulgent society to the poet. Perhaps it is just as well they are not. Opportunities for sympathy are no less precious or necessary to him than opportunities for solitude, and it cannot be denied that through the complex network of mutual ties and obligations woven in the course of earning a livelihood they are most easily and naturally secured.

Sangharakshita
Advice to a Young Poet

THE JOYS OF SOLITUDE

*I*f the mind is not at peace, neither beasts of burden nor possessions are of service, neither palaces nor pavilions bring any cheer. This lonely house is but a tiny hut, but I somehow love it. I naturally feel ashamed when I go to the capital and must beg, but when I return and sit here I feel pity for those still attached to the world of dust. Should anyone doubt the truth of my words, let him look to the fishes and the birds. Fish do not weary of the water, but unless one is a fish one does not know why. Birds long for the woods, but unless one is a bird one does not know why. The joys of solitude are similar. Who could understand them without having lived here?

Kamo no Chomei
An account of my hut

I SAW IN LOUISIANA A LIVE-OAK GROWING

I saw in Louisiana a live-oak growing,
All alone stood it, and the moss hung down
    from the branches,
Without any companion it grew there
    uttering joyous leaves of dark green,
And its look, rude, unbending, lusty, made
    me think of myself.
But I wonder'd how it could utter joyous
    leaves standing alone there without its
    friend near, for I knew I could not,
And I broke off a twig with a certain
    number of leaves upon it, and twined
    around it a little moss,
And brought it away, and I have placed it in
    sight, in my room,
It is not needed to remind me as of my
    own dear friends,
(For I believe lately I think of little else
    than of them),
Yet it remains to me a curious token, it
    makes me think of manly love;

For all that, and though the live-oak glistens
    there in Louisiana solitary in a wide flat
    space,
Uttering joyous leaves all its life without a
    friend a lover near,
I know very well I could not.

                                        Walt Whitman

THE DAFFODILS

I wander'd lonely as a cloud
    That floats on high o'er vales and hills,
When all at once I saw a crowd,
    A host of golden daffodils,
Beside the lake, beneath the trees,
Fluttering and dancing in the breeze.

Continuous as the stars that shine
    And twinkle on the milky way,
They stretch'd in never-ending line
    Along the margin of a bay:
Ten thousand saw I at a glance
Tossing their heads in sprightly dance.

The waves beside them danced, but they
    Out-did the sparkling waves in glee:–
A Poet could not but be gay,
    In such a jocund company!
I gazed – and gazed – but little thought
What wealth the show to me had brought;

For oft, when on my couch I lie
   In vacant or in pensive mood,
They flash upon that inward eye
   Which is the bliss of solitude;
And then my heart with pleasure fills,
And dances with the daffodils.

William Wordsworth

ZARATHUSTRA'S DOWN-GOING

When Zarathustra was thirty years old, he left his home and the lake of his home and went into the mountains. Here he had the enjoyment of his spirit and his solitude and he did not weary of it for ten years. But at last his heart turned – and one morning he rose with the dawn, stepped before the sun, and spoke to it thus:

Great star! What would thy happiness be, if you had not those for whom you shine!

You have come up here to my cave for ten years: you would have grown weary of your light and of this journey, without me, my eagle and my serpent.
But we waited for you every morning, took from you your superfluity and blessed you for it.
Behold! I am weary of my wisdom, like a bee that has gathered too much honey; I need hands outstretched to take it.

I should like to give it away and distribute
    it, until the wise among men have again
    become happy in their folly and the poor
    happy in their wealth.
To that end, I must descend into the depths:
    as you do at evening, when you go
    behind the sea and bring light to the
    underworld too, superabundant star!
Like you, I must go down – as men, to
    whom I want to descend, call it.
So bless me then, tranquil eye, that can behold
    without envy even an excessive happiness!
Bless the cup that wants to overflow, that
    the waters may flow golden from him
    and bear the reflection of your joy over
    all the world!
Behold! This cup wants to be empty again,
    and Zarathustra wants to be man again.
Thus began Zarathustra's down-going.

F.W.Nietzsche
Thus Spoke Zarathustra

THE TREE-ROOTMAN'S PRACTICE

The Blessed One praised roots of trees
As one of the dependencies;
Can he that loves secludedness
Find such another dwelling place?

Secluded at the roots of trees
And guarded well by deities
He lives in true devotedness
Nor covets any dwelling place.

And when the tender leaves are seen
Bright red at first, then turning green,
And then to yellow as they fall,
He sheds belief once and for all

In permanence. Tree roots have been
Bequeathed by him; secluded scene
No wise man will disdain at all
For contemplating rise and fall.

Buddhaghosa
Visuddhmagga

ALONENESS

*E*ach of us is unique: we have our own particular history, our own way of behaving, of feeling, and of thinking. In the soil of our essential aloneness lie these seeds of our nascent individuality, which can be cultivated through spiritual training and practice, and which can manifest as ever higher levels of mental clarity, emotional positivity, and freedom of action.

On the basis of accepting our essential solitude we can begin to recognize all the layers and levels of conditioning that have fashioned our thoughts and beliefs. Thus we can begin to think for ourselves, reflect with reason upon our own unique experience. This process of clarification will be greatly enhanced by meditation, through which we can develop a more concentrated and effective mind.

Grasping our essential solitude we can begin to develop ethical autonomy. Rather than merely conforming to social norms we start to take responsibility for our actions – to move our lives in the direction we ourselves want them to go, and to judge our own and others' actions by our own considered values, and in the light of our own deepest experience and vision, rather than by the received values of any group.

Having a sense of our own aloneness and independence, not needing the approval of others, we can also begin to develop fearlessness. We know all the time that, if need be, we can and will go it alone rather than sacrificing our integrity to the judgements of others. Such a state of positive aloneness is in fact the root of emotional freedom, and that is the basis of real friendship. It is the state from which we begin to develop 'independent', autonomous emotional positivity. We can cultivate metta: non-exclusive feelings of loving-kindness, through which we can empathize with all living beings rather than seeking to bind ourselves in psychological dependence on one particular living being. Taking up meditation practices such as the metta bhavana, we learn to develop metta more systematically. Thus we begin to develop in ourselves the emotional warmth and independence which is the prerequisite for strong, healthy friendships.

In such ways, the recognition and acceptance of our fundamental aloneness is the starting point for the path of higher human development: the spiritual life.

Kulananda
'Solitude: a fact of life', Golden Drum

NO NEWS

My hut lies in the middle of a dense forest;
Every year the green ivy grows longer.
No news of the affairs of men,
Only the occasional song of a woodcutter.
The sun shines and I mend my robe;
When the moon comes out I read Buddhist
    poems.
I have nothing to report, my friends.
If you want to find the meaning, stop
    chasing after so many things.

Ryokan

A SOLITARY RETREAT

waking up
between Africa and Europe
the Mediterranean
and the Atlantic

between
the sea and the ocean
in a mountain hut

the sun's times
summer breeze
the earth crawling
with life

nowhere to go

but upwards
the dangerous pathway

through clouds and
the stars

to be given
a glimpse
of bliss

of the blazing flames

'colder and purer
than snows
and the dawn'

Sridevi

BAMBOO GROVE HOUSE

I sit alone in the dark bamboos
Play my lute and sing and sing
Deep in the woods where no one knows I
    am
But the bright moon comes and shines on
    me there.

Wang Wei

SUFFICIENT SPACE

*T*here is commonly sufficient space about us. Our horizon is never quite at our elbows. The thick wood is not just at our door, nor the pond, but somewhat is always clearing, familiar and worn by us, appropriated and fenced in some way, and reclaimed from Nature. For what reason have I this vast range and circuit, some square miles of unfrequented forest, for my privacy, abandoned to me by men? My nearest neighbor is a mile distant, and no house is visible from any place but the hill-tops within half a mile of my own. I have my horizon bounded by woods all to myself; a distant view of the railroad where it touches the pond on the one hand, and of the fence which skirts the woodland road on the other. But for the most part it is as solitary where I live as on the prairies. It is as much Asia or Africa as New England. I have, as it were, my own sun and moon and stars, and a little world all to myself. At night there was never a traveller passed my house, or knocked at my door, more than if I were the first or last man; unless it were in the spring, when at long intervals some came from the village to fish for pouts, – they plainly fished much more in the Walden Pond of their own natures, and baited their hooks with darkness, – but they soon retreated, usually with light baskets, and left 'the world to darkness and to me', and the black kernel of the night was never profaned by any human neighborhood. I believe that men are generally still a little afraid of the dark, though the witches are all hung, and Christianity and candles have been introduced.

Yet I experienced sometimes that the most sweet and tender, the most innocent and encouraging society may be found in any natural object, even for the poor misanthrope and most melancholy man. There can be no very black melancholy to him who lives in the midst of Nature and has his senses still. There was never yet such a storm but it was Aeolian music to a healthy and innocent ear. Nothing can rightly compel a simple and brave man to a vulgar sadness. While I enjoy the friendship of the seasons I trust that nothing can make life a burden to me. ...

I have never felt lonesome, or in the least oppressed by a sense of solitude, but once, and that was a few weeks after I came to the woods, when, for an hour, I doubted if the near neighborhood of man was not essential to a serene and healthy life. To be alone was something unpleasant. But I was at the same time conscious of a slight insanity in my mood, and seemed to foresee my recovery. In the midst of a gentle rain while these thoughts prevailed, I was suddenly sensible of such sweet and beneficent society in Nature, in the very pattering of the drops, and in every sound and sight around my house, an infinite and unaccountable friendliness all at once like an atmosphere sustaining me, as made the fancied advantages of human neighborhood insignificant, and I have never thought of them since.

H.D. Thoreau
Walden

SOLITUDE

Happy the man, whose wish and care
A few paternal acres bound,
Content to breathe his native air
   In his own ground.

Whose herds with milk, whose fields with
    bread,
Whose flocks supply him with attire;
Whose trees in summer yield him shade,
   In winter fire.

Blest, who can unconcern'dly find
Hours, days, and years, slide soft away
In health of body, peace of mind,
   Quiet by day,

Sound sleep by night; study and ease
Together mixt, sweet recreation,
And innocence, which most does please
   With meditation.

Thus let me live, unseen, unknown;
Thus unlamented let me die;
Steal from the world, and not a stone
   Tell where I lie.

Alexander Pope

THE HAPPINESS OF SOLITUDE.
THE HERMIT'S HISTORY

Prince Rasselas and his sister are travelling with Imlac in quest of someone who is truly happy.

They came on the third day, by the direction of the peasants, to the hermit's cell: it was a cavern in the side of a mountain, overshadowed with palm-trees, at such a distance from the cataract that nothing more was heard than a gentle uniform murmur, such as composed the mind to pensive meditation, especially when it was assisted by the wind whistling among the branches. The first rude essay of nature had been so much improved by human labour that the cave contained several apartments, appropriated to different uses, and often afforded lodging to travellers whom darkness or tempests happened to overtake.

The hermit sat on a bench at the door to enjoy the coolness of the evening. On one side lay a book with pens and papers, on the other mechanical instruments of various kinds. As they approached him unregarded, the princess observed that he had not the countenance of a man that had found, or could teach, the way to happiness.

They saluted him with great respect, which he repaid like a man not unaccustomed to the forms of courts. 'My children,' said he, 'if you have lost your way, you shall be willingly supplied with such conveniences for the night as this cavern will afford. I have all that nature requires, and you will not expect delicacies in a hermit's cell.'

They thanked him, and, entering, were pleased with the neatness and regularity of the place. The hermit set flesh and wine before them, though he fed only upon fruits and water. His discourse was cheerful without levity, and pious without enthusiasm. He soon gained the esteem of his guests, and the princess repented of her hasty censure.

At last Imlac began thus: 'I do not now wonder that your reputation is so far extended; we have heard at Cairo of your wisdom, and came hither to implore your direction for this young man and maiden in the choice of life.'

'To him that lives well,' answered the hermit, 'every form of life is good; nor can I give any other rule for choice than to remove from all apparent evil.'

'He will remove most certainly from evil,' said the prince, 'who shall devote himself to that solitude which you have recommended by your example.'

'I have indeed lived fifteen years in solitude,' said the hermit, 'but have no desire that my example should gain any imitators. In my youth I professed arms, and was raised by degrees to the highest military rank. I have traversed wide countries at the head of my troops, and seen many battles and sieges. At last, being disgusted by the preferment of a younger officer, and finding my vigour beginning to decay, I resolved to close my life in peace, having found the world full of snares, discord, and misery. I had once escaped from the pursuit of the enemy by the shelter of this cavern, and therefore chose it for my final residence. I employed artificers to form it into chambers, and stored it with all that I was likely to want.

'For some time after my retreat, I rejoiced like a tempest-beaten sailor at his entrance into the harbour, being delighted with the sudden change of the noise and hurry of war to stillness and repose. When the pleasure of novelty went away, I employed my hours in examining the plants which grow in the valley and the minerals which I collected from the rocks. But that enquiry is now grown tasteless and irksome. I have been for some time unsettled and distracted: my mind is disturbed with a thousand perplexities of doubt and vanities of imagination which hourly prevail upon me, because I have no opportunities of relaxation or diversion. I am sometimes ashamed to think that I could not secure myself from vice but by retiring from the practice of virtue, and begin to suspect that I was rather impelled by resentment, than led by devotion, into solitude. My fancy riots in scenes of folly, and I lament that I have lost so much and have gained so little. In solitude, if I escape the example of bad men, I want likewise the counsel and conversation of the good. I have been long comparing the evils with the advantages of society, and resolve to return into the world tomorrow. The life of a solitary man will be certainly miserable, but not certainly devout.'

They heard his resolution with surprise, but, after a short pause, offered to conduct him to Cairo. He dug up a considerable treasure which he had hid among the rocks, and accompanied them to the city, on which, as he approached it, he gazed with rapture.

Samuel Johnson
Rasselas

THE STORY OF ASANGA

Nine hundred years after the parinirvana of Gautama Buddha, Arya Asanga was born. In his youth he completed intensive studies in a monastery and in middle life withdrew to a cave to meditate. He determined not to give up his meditation until Maitreya, the Bodhisattva of love and compassion and the Buddha-to-come, manifested himself openly before him.

When, after three years, he had no results, Asanga became discouraged and left his cave. Nearby, he met a man who was making a needle from an iron spike by rubbing it with a piece of cotton. Seeing this, Asanga's patience returned, and he went back to his cave and meditated unceasingly for six more years. Still Maitreya did not manifest himself. Disheartened that he had meditated for nine years without even a sign of success, Asanga again left his cave. Outside he saw how a rock had been completely worn down by single drops of water and the beating wings of passing birds. Again his patience returned, and he resumed his meditation; this time for another three years. But finally, Asanga despaired completely of realizing his aim and set out on the journey to return to his monastery.

On the outskirts of Acinta he saw an old she-dog whose hindquarters were raw and crawling with maggots. He felt great pity for her and wanted to relieve her suffering, but he could not bear to harm the maggots. Instead, he cut a piece of flesh from his own thigh and placed it near the dog. He then put out his tongue and prepared to transfer the larvae one by one, but the sight of the wound was so disgusting that he had to close his eyes. Suddenly, there was a great ringing in his ears, and he opened his eyes. Standing before him, in a magnificent, radiant light, was Maitreya. Despite his joy, Arya Asanga exclaimed without thinking, 'Why did you never come to me during the twelve years I earnestly meditated?'

Maitreya answered, 'I was with you all the time, but you could not see me, because you did not yet have great compassion. If you do not believe me, carry me through the town on your shoulders and try to show me to the people.'

Then Arya Asanga raised Maitreya on his shoulder and carried him through the town, hoping to let everyone see the wonderful Buddha. But no one in the town saw Maitreya, and only one old woman even saw a dog on his shoulder.

A traditional Tibetan story
Geshe Wangyal
The Door of Liberation

PARTING AT MORNING

Round the cape of a sudden came the sea,
And the sun looked over the mountain's
   rim:
And straight was a path of gold for him,
And the need of a world of men for me.

Robert Browning

HIMALAYAN SAGES

Those who have hid themselves on heights
    of snow,
Face to face with the stars and the silver
    moon,
Shall read upon the rocks the Ancient
    Rune
And thus decipher secrets. They shall
    know –
Far from the lips of any earthly lover –
What the mists hide and what the winds
    discover.

And, with grave eyes of wisdom, they shall
    scan –
Pitting terrific wills against th'Unknown,
Wringing its secret out of every stone –
The origin and destiny of man;
Shall see a hundred thousand ages roll
Through one brief instant of the human
    soul.

They shall know utter peace. They shall not
    feel –
Immersed, upon those constellated peaks,
In that deep joy whereof no language
    speaks –
The bitterness and bite of brandished steel.
The tumult of the world rolls on and on:
They shall not hear or heed it. They have
    gone

Afar upon that path which no man
    knoweth
Save who can frailties and passions tread
Underfoot, leave the living and the dead
For snowy heights whereon no green grass
    groweth,
And, meditating there, intensify
Th'electric urge to thrust beyond the 'I'.

Sangharakshita

A LIFE OF SPECIAL LOVE

*T*here will probably always remain some nagging doubts that the hermit life might be self-centred. Some will say: 'Sure! Why shouldn't the hermit be happy? He lives in his own little world! He is content because he is the sole possessor of a universe of which he is himself the center.' The most incredible thing about this statement is that anyone could accept it as a viable formula for happiness. The only possible answer is: 'If you think you can be happy by doing that, why don't you just try it?' The fact is that this is a pure myth. Man is not made in such a way that he can live happily without love. If his life is centered on himself, he may indeed be able to function, but in order to do so his existence is necessarily complicated by his machinery for imposing his will on others. One cannot live a self-centered life simply. Too much cheating is involved – even if one only cheats himself. Supposing a man does live self-centeredly in solitude: he may manage to get by, but he will hardly be content. His discontent will obviously reach out and affect others in some way. He will be mean and unpleasant with them; he will act out his obsessions and inner frenzies upon them. He will project his self-hate on them. He will need them and use them for some irrational purpose, and they will be aware of the fact. Lovelessness cannot be kept hidden, because a loveless life is essentially unhappy, frustrated, and destructive.

The solitary life is then anything but 'lonely' – if by loneliness is meant a loveless and abandoned state. The life of Christian solitude is before all else a life of love, a life of special love. And love is never abstract.

Thomas Merton
Contemplation in a World of Action

ENTERING THE DARK WOOD

*T*hus have I heard. The Exalted One was once staying at Savatthi, in the Jeta Grove, the park of Anathapindika. Now Alavika the Bhikkhuni dressed herself early and, taking bowl and robe, entered Savatthi for food. And when she had gone about Savatthi for it, had broken her fast and returned, she entered the Dark Wood, seeking solitude.

Then Mara the Evil One, desiring to arouse fear, wavering, and dread in her, desiring to make her desist from being alone, went up to her, and addressed her in a verse:

'Ne'er shalt thou find escape while in the world.
What profiteth thee then thy loneliness?
Take the good things of life while yet thou may'st,
Repentance else too late awaiteth thee.'
Then Alavika thought: 'Who now is this, human or non-human, that speaketh this verse? Sure 'tis Mara the Evil One speaketh

it, desirous to arouse in me fear, wavering and dread, desirous to make me desist from my solitude.' And Bhikkhuni Alavika, knowing that 'twas he, replied with a verse:

'There is escape while in the world, and I
Have well attained thereto by insight won.
Thou evil limb of loafing! 'tis not thine
To know that bourne, or how it may be
    reached.
Like spears and jav'lins are the joys of sense,
That pierce and rend the mortal frames of
    us.
These that thou callest "the good things of
    life",
Good of that ilk to me is nothing worth.'

Then Mara, thinking, 'Bhikkhuni Alavika knows me!' vanished thence, sad and dejected.

Songs of the Sisters
(Therigatha)

WISHING FOR A COMPANION

I look far off at T'ien-tai's summit,
Alone and high above the crowding peaks.
Pines and bamboos sing in the wind that
   sways them;
Sea tides wash beneath the shining moon.
I gaze at the mountain's green borders
   below
And discuss philosophy with the white
   clouds.
In the wilderness, mountains and seas are all
   right.
But I wish I had a companion in my search
   for the Way.

Han-shan
Cold Mountain

THESE MORNINGS OF RAIN

These mornings of rain
When the house is cozy
and the phone doesn't ring
and I am alone
though snug
in my daughter's
fire-red robe

These mornings of rain
When my lover's large socks
Cushion my chilly feet
and meditation
has made me one
with the pine tree
outside my door

These mornings of rain
When all noises coming
from the street
have a slippery sound
and the wind whistles

and I have had my cup
of green tea

These mornings
in Fall
When I have slept late
and dreamed
of people I like
in places where we're
obviously on vacation

These mornings
I do not need
my beloved's arms about me
until much later
in the day

I do not need food
I do not need the postperson
I do not need my best friend
to call me
with the latest

on the invasion of Grenada
and her life

I do not need anything

To be warm, to be dry,
to be writing poems again
(after months of distraction
and emptiness!),
to love and be loved
in absentia
is joy enough for me
On these blustery mornings
in a city
that could be wet
from my kisses
I need nothing else
And then again
I need it all.

Alice Walker

CHOICES

Inside the room I see the table laid,
Four chairs, a patch of light the lamp has
made

And people there so deep in tenderness
They could not speak a word of happiness.

Outside I stand and see my shadow drawn
Lengthening the clipped grass of the cared-
    for lawn.

Above, their roof holds half the sky behind.
A dog barks bringing distances to mind.

Comfort, I think, or safety then, or both?
I warm the cold air with my steady breath.

They have designed a way to live and I,
Clothed in confusion, set their choices by:

Though sometimes one looks up and sees
   me there,
Alerts his shadow, pushes back his chair

And, opening windows wide, looks out at
   me
And close past words we stare. It seems that
   he

Urges my darkness, dares it to be freed
Into that room. We need each other's need.

Elizabeth Jennings

CONDITIONS FOR MEDITATION

*T*he third external condition that one must possess if one is to hope for success in the practice of Dhyana [meditation], relates to shelter. A retreat for a follower to be satisfactory must be quiet and free from annoyances and troubles of any kind. There are three kinds of places that are suitable for Dhyana practice: (a) A hermitage in the high and inaccessible mountains. (b) A shack such as would serve a beggar or a homeless monk. These should be at least a mile and a half from a village where even the voice of a cowboy would not reach and where trouble and turmoil would not find it. (c) A bed in a monastery apart from a layman's house.

Grand Master Chih-I
Dhyana for Beginners

WE *ARE* SOLITARY

And to speak of solitude again, it becomes clearer and clearer that fundamentally this is nothing that one can choose or refrain from. We are solitary. We can delude ourselves about this and act as if it were not true. That is all. But how much better it is to recognize that we are alone; yes, even to begin from this realization. It will, of course, make us dizzy; for all points that our eyes used to rest on are taken away from us, there is no longer anything near us, and everything far away is infinitely far. A man taken out of his room and, almost without preparation or transition, placed on the heights of a great mountain range, would feel something like that: an unequalled insecurity, an abandonment to the nameless, would almost annihilate him. He would feel he was falling or think he was being catapulted out into space or exploded into a thousand pieces: what a colossal lie his brain would have to invent in order to catch up with and explain the situation of his senses. That is how all distances, all measures, change for the person who becomes solitary; many of these changes occur suddenly and then, as with the man on the mountaintop, unusual fantasies and strange feelings arise, which seem to grow out beyond all that is bearable. But it is necessary for us to experience that too. We must accept our reality as vastly as we possibly can; everything, even the unprecedented, must be possible within it. This is in the end the only kind of courage required of us: the courage to face the strangest, most unusual, most inexplicable experiences that can meet us.

Rainer Maria Rilke
Letters to a Young Poet
trans. Stephen Mitchell

The Windhorse symbolizes the energy of the enlightened mind carrying the Three Jewels – the Buddha, the Dharma, and the Sangha – to all sentient beings.

Buddhism is one of the fastest growing spiritual traditions in the Western world. Throughout its 2,500-year history, it has always succeeded in adapting its mode of expression to suit whatever culture it has encountered.

Windhorse Publications aims to continue this tradition as Buddhism comes to the West. Today's Westerners are heirs to the entire Buddhist tradition, free to draw instruction from all the many schools and branches. Windhorse publishes works by authors who not only understand the Buddhist tradition but are also familiar with Western culture and the Western mind.

Manuscripts are welcome.

For orders and catalogues contact

Windhorse Publications
11 Park Road
Birmingham
B13 8AB
UK

Windhorse Books
PO Box 574
Newtown
NSW 2042
Australia

Weatherhill Inc
41 Monroe Turnpike
Trumbull
CT 06611
USA

Windhorse Publications is an arm of the Friends of the Western Buddhist Order, which has more than sixty centres on five continents. Through these centres, members of the Western Buddhist Order offer regular programmes of events for the general public and for more experienced students. These include meditation classes, public talks, study on Buddhist themes and texts, and 'bodywork' classes such as t'ai chi, yoga, and massage. The FWBO also runs several retreat centres and the Karuna Trust, a fund-raising charity that supports social welfare projects in the slums and villages of India.

Many FWBO centres have residential spiritual communities and ethical businesses associated with them. Arts activities are encouraged too, as is the development of strong bonds of friendship between people who share the same ideals. In this way the FWBO is developing a unique approach to Buddhism, not simply as a set of techniques, less still as an exotic cultural interest, but as a creatively directed way of life for people living in the modern world.

If you would like more information about the FWBO visit the website at

www.fwbo.org

or write to

London Buddhist Centre
51 Roman Road
London
E2 0HU
UK

Aryaloka Retreat Center
Heartwood Circle
Newmarket
New Hampshire
NH 03857
USA

ALSO FROM WINDHORSE

Compiled by Vidyadevi
REFLECTIONS ON WILDNESS

Wildness. The word evokes open spaces and open hearts. Wildness is about going beyond what the world conventionally requires, touching the mythic dimension of life.

This imaginative and thought-provoking selection draws on the riches of Western literature as well as the wisdom of the Buddhist tradition. It will give you something to dwell on – and dream about.

Don't settle for tame pleasures. Try wildness.

80 pages
ISBN 1 899579 34 6
£4.99/$9.95

Sangharakshita
COMPLETE POEMS 1941–1994

Sangharakshita has dedicated himself to helping people transform their lives not only through his work as a Buddhist teacher but also through the medium of verse, for in his poetry he combines the sensitivity of the poet with the vision born of a life of contemplation and uncompromising spiritual practice.

Here we have the opportunity to listen to a unique voice and to be uplifted by the reflections of an extraordinary person and an accomplished teacher.

528 pages, hardback
ISBN 0 904766 70 5
£17.99/$34.95

Sir Edwin Arnold
THE LIGHT OF ASIA

This inspiring poem by Sir Edwin Arnold
(1832–1904), though written more than a hundred years ago, retains the power to move us in a
way that no prose rendering of the life of the
Buddha can. We cannot but admire the courage,
determination, and self-sacrifice of the Indian
prince who, out of compassion, left his palace to
find a remedy for the sufferings of the world.

192 pages, hardback, with glossary
ISBN 1 899579 19 2
£9.99/$19.95

Sangharakshita
PEACE IS A FIRE

This collection of aphorisms, teachings, and
poems by the pioneering Western Buddhist
Sangharakshita offers instant inspiration to anyone who is ready to have their views challenged
and their mind expanded.

The breadth of the author's thought is well rep-
resented in these sayings which range from art
and literature, through sex and relationships, to
philosophy and religion. His words point beyond
themselves to Reality itself, to the freedom
accessible to all who dare to change.

160 pages, with photographs
ISBN 0 904766 84 5
£6.99/$13.95

Sangharakshita
A STREAM OF STARS:
REFLECTIONS AND APHORISMS

A Stream of Stars is a collection of aphorisms, poems, and writings by the eminent Western Buddhist teacher, Sangharakshita. Encompassing culture and society, relationships and the human condition, these incisive teachings illuminate many aspects of life.

With clarity, insight, and flashes of humour, Sangharakshita provokes us to thought and then to aspiration: an aspiration to true happiness and freedom.

136 pages, with photographs
ISBN 1 899579 08 7
£6.99/$13.95

Stephen Parr (Ananda)
NORTH OF THE FUTURE

In this comprehensive collection Stephen Parr
(Ananda) guides us through the complex webs of
love and family relationships, portraying people
and places with language that is direct, yet far-
reaching in its eloquence.

These are poems of poignancy and humour,
inspired by the Buddhist insights of im-
permanence and interconnectedness.

280 pages, hardback
ISBN 0 904766 76 4
£11.99/$23.95

Sangharakshita
THE CALL OF THE FOREST
AND OTHER POEMS

Profound contemplation of nature and spiritual vision feature prominently in this collection of Sangharakshita's recent poems. Here we can see how the practice of Buddhism combines with the writing of poetry. Both require the cultivation of an intense sympathy with others, which forms the basis of the essential Buddhist virtue of loving-kindness.

56 pages
ISBN 1 899579 24 9
£7.99/$15.95